My Notes

My Notes

Make
Halloween
Great Again

My Notes

Make
Halloween
Great Again

My Notes

Make Halloween Great Again

My Notes

Make
Halloween
Great Again

My Notes

Make
Halloween
Great Again

My Notes

Make
Halloween
Great Again

My Notes

My Notes

My Notes

My Notes

My Notes

My Notes

My Notes

Make
Halloween
Great Again

My Notes

Make Halloween Great Again

My Notes

My Notes

My Notes

Make
Halloween
Great Again

My Notes

Make
Halloween
Great Again

My Notes

My Notes

Make
Halloween
Great Again

My Notes

Make Halloween Great Again
Make Halloween Great Again

My Notes

Make
Halloween
Great Again

My Notes

My Notes

Make Halloween Great Again

My Notes

My Notes

My Notes

My Notes

Make Halloween Great Again

My Notes

My Notes

Make
Halloween
Great Again

My Notes

Make
Halloween
Great Again

My Notes

Make
Halloween
Great Again

My Notes

Make
Halloween
Great Again

My Notes

Make
Halloween
Great Again

My Notes

My Notes

My Notes

Make
Halloween
Great Again

My Notes

My Notes

Make
Halloween
Great Again

My Notes

My Notes

My Notes

Make
Halloween
Great Again

My Notes

Make Halloween Great Again

My Notes

Make
Halloween
Great Again

My Notes

Make
Halloween
Great Again

My Notes

My Notes

My Notes

My Notes

My Notes

Make
Halloween
Great Again

My Notes

Make Halloween Great Again

My Notes

Make
Halloween
Great Again

My Notes

My Notes

My Notes

Make
Halloween
Great Again

My Notes

Make
Halloween
Great Again

My Notes

Make
Halloween
Great Again

My Notes

Make
Halloween
Great Again

My Notes

Make Halloween Great Again
Make Halloween Great Again

My Notes

Make
Halloween
Great Again

My Notes

Make
Halloween
Great Again

My Notes

Make
Halloween
Great Again

My Notes

Make
Halloween
Great Again

My Notes

Make
Halloween
Great Again

My Notes

My Notes

Make
Halloween
Great Again

My Notes

My Notes

My Notes

Make
Halloween
Great Again

My Notes

Make
Halloween
Great Again

My Notes

My Notes

Make
Halloween
Great Again

My Notes

My Notes

My Notes

Make
Halloween
Great Again

My Notes

Make
Halloween
Great Again

My Notes

Make
Halloween
Great Again

My Notes

My Notes

My Notes

My Notes

Make
Halloween
Great Again

My Notes

Make
Halloween
Great Again

My Notes

My Notes

My Notes

My Notes

Make Halloween Great Again

My Notes

Make
Halloween
Great Again

My Notes

Make
Halloween
Great Again

My Notes

My Notes

Make Halloween Great Again

My Notes

My Notes

My Notes

Make
Halloween
Great Again

My Notes

Make
Halloween
Great Again

My Notes

My Notes

Make
Halloween
Great Again

My Notes

My Notes

Make
Halloween
Great Again

My Notes

Make Halloween Great Again

www.ingramcontent.com/pod-product-compliance
Lightning Source LLC
LaVergne TN
LVHW021053100526
838202LV00083B/5837
* 9 7 8 3 3 4 7 1 7 0 4 6 9 *